THE STORY OF THE CHRISTMAS TRUCE

SILENT NIGHT, *Holy Night*

AS NARRATED BY WALTER CRONKITE

ILLUSTRATED BY ROBERT T. BARRETT

SHADOW
MOUNTAIN

MORMON
TABERNACLE
CHOIR

The Mormon Tabernacle Choir would like to acknowledge the efforts of Stephen Wunderli, David Warner, and Mack Wilberg in preparing the script for this story. The original musical score for this presentation was composed by Mack Wilberg, associate music director of the Choir. In researching this remarkable story, the writers relied heavily on Stanley Weintraub's Silent Night: The Story of the World War I Christmas Truce *(New York: Free Press, 2001) and on the BBC documentary:* WWI. *It is from these two sources that the quotes from soldiers and eyewitnesses came. Interviews with children and grandchildren of soldiers who fought in World War I also provided details for the emotions and settings described in the story. Other sources for the story include Paul Johnson,* A History of the American People *(New York: HarperCollins Publishers, 1998); John Keegan,* The First World War *(New York: A. Knopf, 1999); Winston Churchill,* The Great Republic *(New York: Random House, 2000); and the Imperial War Museum in London. The photographs used throughout the book are owned by members of the Mormon Tabernacle Choir and are used with permission. The soldiers pictured in the photographs served in World War I and are ancestors of Choir members.*

SHADOW MOUNTAIN is a registered trademark of Deseret Book Company.

Visit us at mormontabernaclechoir.org

Library of Congress Cataloging-in-Publication Number
2003011815   ISBN 1-59038-166-1

Printed in the United States of America   42316-0096R
Inland Press, Menomonee Falls, WI

10   9   8   7   6   5   4   3   2

INTRODUCTION

The Christmases of today seem a far cry from 1914. But the themes expressed in the trenches and those that graced the headlines of that year are still hauntingly familiar. This story, although compressed, is a true story. The events are documented in newspapers and in letters home from soldiers on both sides. Their stories have been retold for generations. They were shared again by Walter Cronkite to more than eighty thousand concertgoers, attending four concerts over four days, at the Conference Center in Salt Lake City. Hundreds of requests for the script have led to its publication in this book.

We dedicate this book to those who gave their lives in World War I and to all those who have served their country.

T HE 1900S, THE FINAL CENTURY of the recent millennium, brought unprecedented possibilities and promise.

The children of these hundred years would see more improvement in the human condition than ever before in the world's history.

Advances in medicine, science, and industry would all but eradicate disease, extend human life, open a dialogue among the peoples of the earth, and lift them into the vast reaches of space.

But these hardly seemed like possibilities as the Christmas of 1914 drew near.

The nations of Europe were at war. Anxious to expand and defend their borders, they summoned their best and brightest to the battle-front. Young men answered by the millions.

A NINETEEN-YEAR-OLD German boy left his job in London to enlist in the German army. English boys working and studying in Hamburg and Paris returned to London, put on their uniforms, and went back to fire upon former friends.

SECRETARY OF WAR, Lord Kitchener, expanded the British army overnight by allowing schoolmates to enlist together.

The tragedy of these battalions was no more evident than at Somme, France. Hundreds of villages on both sides lost almost all their young men in a single battle. The little paybook that every British soldier carried included a last will and testament. Thousands of these booklets were collected from the bodies of young boys, many reading simply, "I leave everything to my mother."

WITH HARDLY A BACKWARD GLANCE, the promise of youth was poured into the blind and futile aggression known as the Great War, World War I.

The new century brought a new kind of warfare. Field commanders quickly realized that digging in was the only way to survive the sweep of machine-gun fire.

THE GERMAN ARMY HAD MARCHED across Belgium before being stopped at Flanders Field. Some sixty yards away, British, French, and Belgian troops languished in trenches infested with rats and lice; pelted with freezing rain and shrapnel. As temperatures dropped, disease took hold. Snipers picked off any who raised their heads above the earthen wall. The war was but four months old, each side losing thousands a day, both to bullets and that silent, common enemy: influenza.

Between the opposing trenches was an area about the width of a football field: No Man's Land. Littered with barbed wire and frozen corpses, it was a sobering reminder of what the future might bring. Soldiers who survived later recalled their dead brothers being gathered up and stacked like cords of wood. By war's end, over ten million would be lost.

Not surprisingly, given the circumstances, most of the soldiers were religious; and many were Christian. On Sundays, communion was passed in trenches on both sides, often to the sound of church bells ringing in nearby villages. The occasional hymn was sung, and youthful voices were heard across enemy lines.

By December, the war slowed and hopes for a quick resolution faded away. As the soldiers contemplated their desperate situation, nights grew long and hearts yearned for peace.

December twenty-third. A group of German soldiers quietly moved to the ruins of a bombed-out monastery. There, they held their Christmas service.

LATER ON THAT NIGHT, a few Christmas trees, *Tannenbaums* as they were called, began to appear along the German fortifications, their tiny candles flickering in the night.

Across the way, British soldiers took an interest in those lights as they sang together the carols of their youth. Word spread, and heads peeked cautiously over sandbags at the now thousands of Tannenbaums glowing like Christmas stars.

Two British officers ventured over to the German line and, against orders, arranged a Christmas truce. But the negotiation was a mere formality by then. Up and down the trenches men from both sides already had begun crossing the line to join the celebration.

Lieutenant Sir Edward Hulse "assaulted" the enemy with music. In a letter to his mother he wrote, "We are going to give the enemy every conceivable song . . . from carols to Tipperary."

The Germans responded with a Christmas concert of their own. It was not long before the cold air rang with everything from "Good King Wenceslas" to "Auld Lang Syne."

For the next two days, those tidings continued to spring from the hearts of common men who shared the common bond of Christmas.

FURTHER DOWN THE LINE, a German violinist stood atop his parapet, framed against the skeletons of bare trees and shattered fortifications. Delicately perched in this desolate landscape, his cold fingers conveyed the poignant beauty of Handel's *Largo*.

Whatever the spirit of Christmas had been before that hour, it was now, above all, the spirit of hope, of peace.

A British war correspondent reported that later the soldiers heard a clear voice singing the beloved French carol, "O Holy Night." The singer: Victor Granier of the Paris Opera. The night watch must have lifted their eyes toward the heavens as they heard his plaintive call.

C HRISTMAS DAY DAWNED over the muddy fields, and both sides cautiously picked their way through the barbed wire. Side by side they buried their dead.

A GERMAN OFFICER KNOWN ONLY AS THOMAS gave Lieutenant Hulse a Christmas gift: a Victoria cross and letter which had belonged to an English captain. Lieutenant Hulse responded by giving the German officer his silk scarf. One German retrieved a photograph of himself in uniform and asked his former enemies to post it to his sister in Liverpool.

Men who had shot at each other only days before gathered in a sacred service for their fallen brothers. Prayers were offered, and the twenty-third Psalm was read:

> *The Lord is my shepherd; I shall not want.*
>
> *He maketh me to lie down in green pastures: he leadeth me beside the still waters.*
>
> *He restoreth my soul: he leadeth me in the paths of righteousness for his name's sake.*
>
> *Yea, though I walk through the valley of the shadow of death, I will fear no evil: for thou art with me; thy rod and thy staff they comfort me.*
>
> *Thou preparest a table before me in the presence of mine enemies: thou anointest my head with oil; my cup runneth over.*
>
> *Surely goodness and mercy shall follow me all the days of my life: and I will dwell in the house of the Lord for ever.*

Nineteen-year-old Arthur Pelham-Burn, who hoped to study for the ministry after the war ended, remembered: "The Germans formed up on one side, the English on the other, the officers standing in front, every head bared. Yes, I think it is a sight one will never see again."

As the Christmas of 1914 drew to a close, soldiers who had sung together, played together, and prayed together, returned to their trenches. They must have felt reluctant to let the common ground between them become No Man's Land again. But as the darkness fell around them, a lone voice floated across the few yards of earth on which they had stood together. In the true spirit of Christmas, one voice, then another, joined in. Soon, the whole world seemed to be singing. And, for a brief moment, the sound of peace was a carol every soul knew by heart.

Silent night! Holy night!

All is calm, all is bright

Round yon virgin mother and Child.

Holy Infant, so tender and mild,

Sleep in heavenly peace;

Sleep in heavenly peace.

Silent night! Holy night!

Shepherds quake at the sight!

Glories stream from heaven afar;

Heav'nly hosts sing Alleluia!

Christ, the Savior, is born!

Christ, the Savior, is born!

Silent night! Holy night!

Son of God, love's pure light

Radiant beams from thy holy face,

With the dawn of redeeming grace,

Jesus, Lord, at thy birth;

Jesus, Lord, at thy birth.

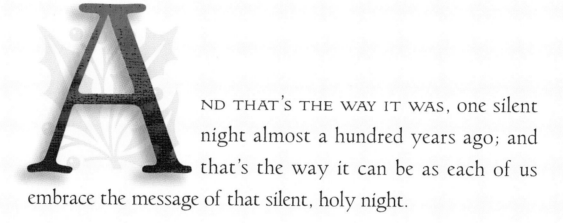

And that's the way it was, one silent night almost a hundred years ago; and that's the way it can be as each of us embrace the message of that silent, holy night.

AFTERWORD

THERE ARE MANY DETAILS IN WAR STORIES; some contribute to good story-telling, while others are just interesting. Omitting some of these details was perhaps the most difficult part of assembling this true story. Each detail brought gravity to a heavy war and made the Christmas truce all that more profound. Throughout December, gifts—English puddings and German chocolate—were heaved from trench to trench. A German boot exploded in an English trench, stuffed with sausages, chocolate, and cigars. There were soccer games in No Man's Land. A British soldier captured a rabbit, and soldiers from both sides contributed tins of vegetables and meat to make a batch of Christmas stew. It hardly seemed possible at the time that the war would last so long.

But the squabble turned into a long, brutal war. The industrial revolution spawned machinery capable of killing thousands at a time. In the end, not only would ten million die but the tenuous peace would also foster a bitterness that festered until the Second World War began.

Still, for a time, young Londoners who had befriended German waiters and German patrons of French operas saw the war as something temporary. They didn't really hate each other in the first few months. It was only out of duty that they fought. So when an opportunity to celebrate a common holiday arose, so did the men from their trenches.

The guns were silent for a day. And when soldiers from both sides returned to their trenches after Christmas and the command to resume was issued, they would fire only at the clouds. The war would not continue until replacements were rotated in.